Contents

I   *Signs Around Us*

The world we live in is full of signs. Every day, we probably look at dozens of them without even thinking about it. They are so common that we take them for granted.

A sign is an easy way of telling us something which we might need to know. Instead of using words, we use a picture, because it is so much quicker to recognise a picture than to read words.

Look at these two signs. Which one is easiest to understand quickly?

Signs save us time. Some signs are so simple that we hardly think of them as signs at all. Think of the signs we use in mathematics: $+$ $-$ $\times$ and $\div$. Or even the full stops we use to show that a sentence has ended.

The space at the start of this line told you that a new paragraph had started. It all seems so obvious. But if no one had told us these things when we were younger, we would not have understood.

Signs are more necessary these days because so many people travel abroad. Words have to be translated from one language to another but pictures do not. So, if the three signs below are used on public lavatories, most people from most countries will understand what they mean:

This book makes use of signs to save you time. If you see a word in heavy type **like this** you can look up what it means on page 31. This sign: ▶ shows there is a quotation.

Our actions can also be signs. Think of deaf and dumb people who talk in sign language, or putting your hand up to answer a question. If we do not say *please* or *thank you*, it could be a sign that we are rude – or just lazy! If you were sitting talking in the classroom it might be a sign that you were not concentrating on the lesson.

Signs help us to understand other people and the world in which we live. So, if a man walked through a door marked

it could be a sign that he was

stupid   or   forgetful!

Signs, Symbols and Stories

J F Aylett

Hodder & Stoughton
LONDON SYDNEY AUCKLAND

Acknowledgements

The publisher would like to thank the Bible Society for the extracts from *The Good News Bible* published by The Bible Societies and Collins, © American Bible Society 1966, 1971, 1976; Janet Williams, Anna Hinks and Tom Jackson and their teacher Mrs Jeanette Brooks of Rotherfield County Primary School, Sussex, for the drawings of God.

The publishers would like to thank the following for their permission to reproduce copyright illustrations:

Andes Press Agency/Carlos Reyes, pp. 14R, 16L; APA Photo Agency, p. 29; Barnaby's Picture Library, pp. 16R, 25, 28; British Library, p. 8R; Dem Amirakis Studio, p. 19; Sally & Richard Greenhill, p. 23; Greenpeace/ Vennemann, p. 7; Sonia Halliday & Laura Lushington, p. 8L; Sonia Halliday Photographs, p. 24R; Michael Holford, p. 26R; Rex Features Ltd, pp. 14L, 22R, 26L; Royal Commonwealth Society, p. 24L; Peter Sanders, p. 22L; Ronald Sheridan's Ancient Art & Architecture Collection, p. 11; Juliette Soester, p. 20; Topham Picture Library, p. 12.

I would like to thank my wife for her considerable assistance with the research for this book. In addition, I should like to thank the following for their help: the Right Reverend the Bishop of Militoupolis, Timotheos; Maurice Chandler, CBE, Honorary Consul of Kiribati; the Very Rev. Dr George D Dragas; Terry Barringer of the Royal Commonwealth Society; the Hindu Centre, London; the Buddhist Society; the Islamic Cultural Centre; the Vedic Society; Japan Information Centre; the Commonwealth Institute; Middle Eastern Christian Outreach; the Turkish Tourist Office; the Embassy of the People's Republic of China; and the Indonesian Embassy.

J.F.A.

© 1989 J F Aylett

First published in Great Britain 1989
Third impression 1993

British Library Cataloguing in Publication Data

Aylett, J.F. (John F.)
  Signs and symbols.
  1. Religions   For schools
  I. Title   II. Series
  291

ISBN 0–340–49051–9

Typeset in 11 on 13pt Plantin Roman by Taurus Graphics. Abingdon, Oxon. Printed and bound in Hong Kong for the educational publishing division of Hodder and Stoughton Ltd, Mill Road, Dunton Green, Sevenoaks, Kent by Colorcraft Ltd.

1 a) Look at the drawing above. The artist has included nine signs in the circles. Write each number on a separate line, then write down what you think the signs stand for. If you are not sure, at least make a guess.

b) There are some *other* signs in the main picture. Draw at least one of them and explain what it means.

2 a) Give at least two reasons why we use signs.

b) Think of at least one reason why signs can cause problems.

3 Draw three signs which you can see in your town. Explain what they mean.

4 a) Draw any signs you can see in your school.

b) Which sign do you think is least easy to understand? Explain how you decided.

5 a) Design a sign for the front of your religious studies book. Draw it in your book, not on the cover.

b) Compare your sign with those of other people in your group. How can you decide whose sign is best?

2 Identity Discs

However simple signs are, we still have to learn what they mean.

Look at the sign above. A heart with an arrow through it is usually a sign of love. If you add initials at each end of the arrow it will mean that those two people love each other – or that at least one of them is in love!

But why does it mean that? It is only because we are used to it. If you think about it, it could be a sign of hatred or death. After all, an arrow is a weapon; one person could want to kill another person. We only know it doesn't mean this because we have learned it.

The other picture above is a good example of this. It has a heart in it but it doesn't mean love. It is the symbol of the British Heart Foundation which raises money for heart research. The lines below the heart stand for the beat of a person's heart. So a long straight line would be a sign that a person was dead.

Look at the girl in the picture above. Her dress is a sign that she is a Brownie and the badges on it are a sign that she has passed various tests. The badge on her tie is a *symbol* of the promises she has made. She has promised to do her duty to God, to serve the Queen and help other people, and to keep the Brownie Law. She wears the badge so that other people will know this.

Many people wear badges like this to show that they belong to a club or organisation. Sometimes, people put stickers on their car windows for the same reason.

The picture above shows the symbol of CND – the Campaign for **Nuclear Disarmament.** The circle contains the shapes used to symbolise the letters N and D in semaphore.

This tells you what the symbol stands for but it may have an extra meaning for certain people. For instance, think of someone who had been injured when a nuclear bomb was dropped in the war.

Some people would say that the ship above is a symbol. It is used by an organisation which tries to stop **pollution** and protect wildlife. Some people think it is just a nuisance but its supporters believe it is a symbol of peace and caring for other creatures on our planet.

Religions, too, have symbols. People often use them so that others will know they are members of that religion. But they are more than just shapes. Each has a deeper meaning which means more to a follower of that religion. The symbols also affect people's feelings so they may mean slightly different things to different people.

THE CROSS is a symbol of CHRISTIANITY

The cross is the symbol of the death of Jesus. Christians believe he died for the sake of everyone on earth. It also reminds Christians that God loved Jesus and raised him from the dead. So it is a symbol of God's love for everyone.

THE STAR OF DAVID is the symbol of JUDAISM

Jews have only been using this symbol for two or three centuries and it has no religious meaning. But it does have great emotional meaning. The Germans made Jews wear this badge as a sign of shame in the Second World War so that everyone knew they were Jewish. Polish Jews replied by making them out of the most costly material they could get. It was a symbol of their pride in being Jewish.

THE KHANDA is the symbol of SIKHISM

The two-edged sword is called the Khanda. It is a symbol of God's concern for truth and justice. The other two swords stand for God's power, while the circle is a sign of the Unity of God.

THE WHEEL OF THE LAW is the symbol of BUDDHISM

The rim of the wheel stands for the cycle of birth, death and rebirth which Buddhists believe people are tied to by desire. Each spoke represents an action which a Buddhist should practise to escape from the wheel. At its centre is a point where there is peace; when a Buddhist reaches this, he or she will not be reborn. They call this **Nirvana**.

1 Match up each religion with the correct symbol from the right.

Christianity	the Khanda
Sikhism	the Cross
Buddhism	the Star of David
Judaism	the Wheel of the Law

2 a) Write down what each of these words reminds you of: love; hate; happiness; caring; sharing; and sadness. For instance, sadness may remind you of a pet which has died.

b) In pairs, ask your partner to read out each answer in turn to (a). Put them in a different order! Try to work out which word each answer matches up with.

c) Draw a good symbol for the idea of sharing things. Explain why you chose that symbol.

3 a) Choose any religious symbol and write down what it might mean to a believer in that religion.

b) What else might this symbol remind a believer about?

4 a) Why do you think the following use signs:
British Rail; banks; television companies; and clothes manufacturers?

b) The four groups in (a) change their signs from time to time. Why do you think religious symbols do not change?

3 Once Upon a Time . . .

Sometimes, as we have seen, symbols can get quite difficult to work out. Young children find it especially hard to understand words like 'good' and 'evil' because they are symbols for difficult ideas. So adults tell them stories to help them to understand. Symbols are used in these stories. Many of them begin in the same way...

> **Note:** The words shown in *italics* are symbols. (For instance, *children* are a symbol of innocence.)

▶ Once upon a time, there was a *young and handsome* knight in bright armour with a magic sword called Ascalon. He travelled to distant lands in search of adventure.

One of these lands was ruled by a king who had only *one* child, a *young* and beautiful daughter. A huge, man-eating *dragon* had come to live in a lake in the kingdom. Every day, it headed for the town, seizing hold of any living thing it could. The people were terrified.

Eventually, the people did a deal with the dragon. Every morning they left two *fat lambs* outside the city gates. In return, the dragon left the people alone. Unfortunately, the supply of lambs ran out.

The dragon was furious. It liked lambs. But it liked tender, juicy *children*, too. So, next, one of the children was chosen instead each day to be left to be fed to the dragon. One day, the princess was the child chosen to die. Outside the gates, she waited.

As the dragon's roar could be heard, up rode the knight on a *white* horse; in his hand, he held his *standard*.

'Ride away as fast as you can!' shouted the girl. 'No one can survive the burning flame which comes from the dragon's jaws. Don't risk your life trying to save me!'

But the knight did not listen. He turned on the dragon and drove his lance into its throat. 'Undo your **sash** and tie it round the dragon's throat,' the knight told the princess. When she had done this, she led the dragon to the market-place and it followed *as quietly as a lamb.*

The people could not believe it; they thought it must be *witchcraft.* But the knight called out that he was a Christian and that God had given him the *strength to tame the dragon.*

Then, he cut off the dragon's head and later that day, the people became Christians. The king offered the knight *his daughter's hand in marriage* and the right to be his heir. But the knight declined and rode off in search of other brave deeds.

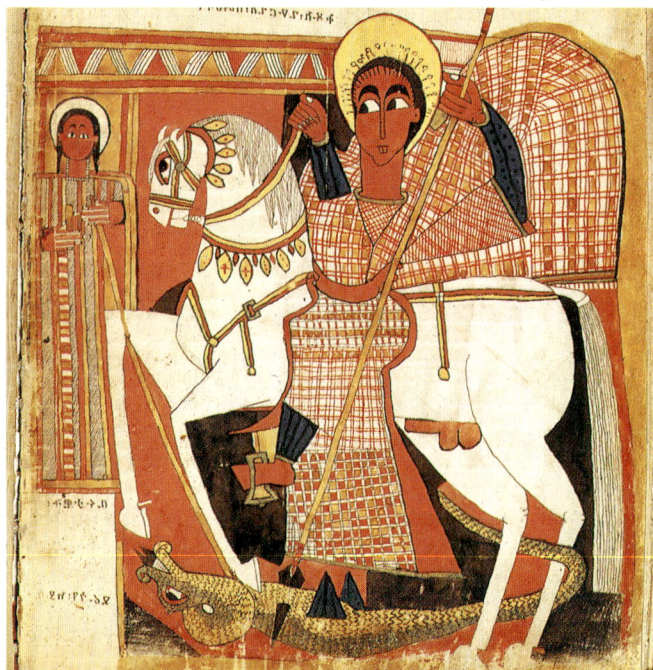

St George is now the **patron saint** of England. His standard is used as the English flag and is flown on St George's Day (23 April). The two pictures on this page show him in a stained glass window (above, left) and in an Ethiopian painting (above).

We know some stories so well that we do not always realise that the people or things in the stories are actually symbols at all. Yet every fairy story you ever heard contains symbols. Sometimes, a person is a symbol of evil, like the wicked witch in *Snow White*. Sometimes, it is an animal, such as the big, bad wolf.

We have created our own Symbol Land in the picture below. Our artist has included 16 symbols. How many can you spot?
(See question 2.)

1 a) Pick any five symbols from the legend of St George and write down what each one stands for.
b) Which symbols do you find hardest to understand? Try to explain why you find it difficult.
c) What is St George himself a symbol of?

2 a) Look at the drawing above. Write down each symbol you can find on a separate line.
b) Beside each, write down what you think it stands for. (Write it down even if you are not completely sure.)

3 a) Look at the two pictures on page 8. What are the main differences between them? Suggest a reason for these differences.
b) How is the dragon drawn in the lower picture?
c) Why do you think the artist drew it like that? (*Clue:* read the caption.)

4 a) As a group. discuss your answers to question 2. How many symbols did you find?
b) Pick the symbols which most people found. What different meanings were given for them?

4 In the Beginning

Stories can also explain things about the world which are hard to understand. Where did people come from? Where did the world come from? The story below comes from Kiribati in the Pacific Ocean. It is a **creation myth.** In other words, it is a story which tells how the world came into being.

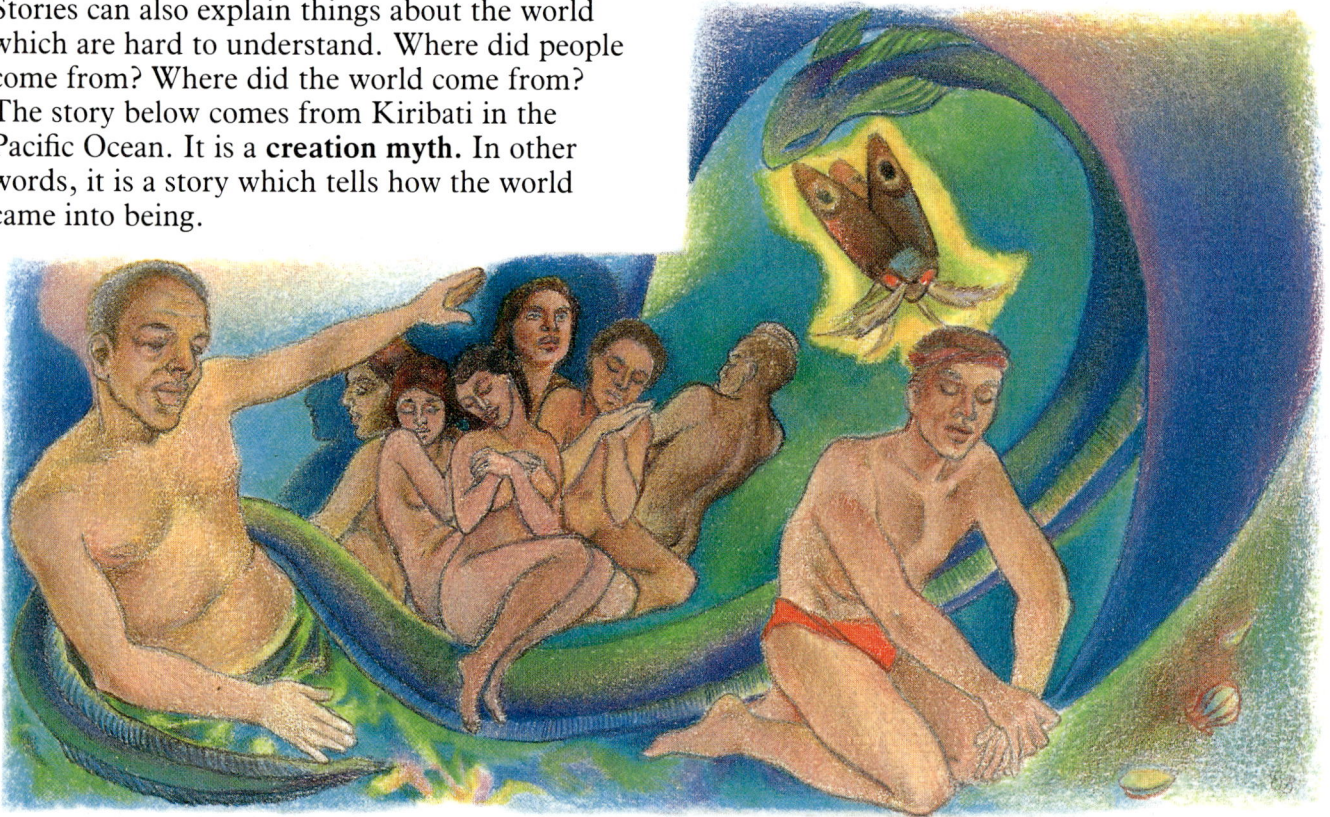

▶ Before there was anything else, there was Nareau the Elder. All around him was darkness and emptiness. There was no food; there was no night and day. So Nareau the Elder sat alone in the darkness.

Gradually, he began to change. Instead of one, he became two: Nareau the Elder and Nareau the Younger. Nareau the Elder spoke.

'My work is nearly done,' he said. 'I have only one thing left to do. I will make a universe for you to practise your skills on.' So he stretched out a hand and created a universe before slowly disappearing.

The earth, sea and sky were still joined together in this universe. So Nareau the Younger knelt on top of the sky, looking for a way in. 'I shall use my magic powers', he said.

He tapped three times on the sky and it opened. Inside, all was pitch black. So Nareau rubbed his fingertips together and there was light – and a tiny, **luminous** moth appeared.

Nareau followed the moth through the opening. Inside, there were people but they were all asleep in the darkness. Nareau called to them and ordered them to stand up and lift the sky, which they did. But the sky stayed fixed to the land. So Nareau sent for Conger Eel, the mighty Lord of the deep sea.

'Greetings, Lord of the Depths,' said Nareau. 'Reach up and lift the sky with your head, and press the land down with your tail.'

So the eel uncoiled his huge body and pressed upwards. Slowly, the great roof of the sky moved upwards as its roots were torn out of the land. Then, Nareau leapt up and grabbed the edge of the sky and pulled it down until it was firmly fastened all round.

A shadow fell over the land and Nareau the Elder reappeared. Nareau the Younger leapt again and killed his father with his magical sword. He took his father's right eye and flung it eastwards where it lit up the sky; it was the sun. The left eye was thrown westwards and became the moon. The ribs of his father he threw upwards and they turned into stars ...

Stories like this one have been told all over the world. Each religion has its own version about how the world began.

The two pictures on this page show scenes from the Kiribati and Christian creation myths. The picture above is from the twelfth century and shows God in the garden of Eden with Adam and Eve. Look carefully at the picture and decide whether you think it shows Adam and Eve before or after the eating of the fruit.

The Christian religion's creation story can be found in chapter 1 of the book of Genesis. In chapter 2, it tells of Adam and Eve, the first man and woman.

Some Christians believe these chapters give a true idea of what really happened when the world began. Others think that these stories are myths, rather like the one on page 10. For them, Adam and Eve were not real people; they are symbols which stand for all people everywhere.

The snake which comes to tempt them is a symbol of evil; and the fruit they eat from the tree is a symbol, too. And the symbols do not end there …

▶ Now the snake was the most cunning animal that the Lord God had made. The snake asked the woman, 'Did God really tell you not to eat fruit from any tree in the garden?'

'We may eat the fruit of any tree in the garden,' the woman answered, 'except the tree in the middle of it. God told us not to eat the fruit of that tree or even touch it; if we do, we will die.'

The snake replied, 'That's not true; you will not die. God said that, because he knows that when you eat it you will be like God and know what is good and what is bad.'

The woman saw how beautiful the tree was and how good its fruits would be to eat, and she thought how wonderful it would be to become wise. So she took some of the fruit and ate it. Then she gave some to her husband, and he also ate it. As soon as they had eaten it, they were given understanding and realised that they were naked; so they sewed fig leaves together and covered themselves.

That evening they heard the Lord God walking in the garden, and they hid from him among the trees. But the Lord God called out to the man, 'Where are you?'

He answered, 'I heard you in the garden; I was afraid and hid from you, because I was naked.'

1 a) Here are four symbols from the story on page 10: darkness; the moth; people asleep; and the eel. Choose any two and explain what they stand for.
   b) Pick out three symbols from the story of Adam and Eve. Explain what each one stands for.
2 a) Is the moth a good symbol for light?
   b) Is a snake a good symbol for evil? Give reasons for each answer.
3 a) Look at the picture above. Write down what you think is happening in the picture. Explain how you decided.
   b) What do you think Christians can learn from the story of Adam and Eve?
4 If you had to explain to a young child about the creation of the world, what symbols would *you* use to stand for these things: the sun; the first sign of animal life; danger; wickedness; and knowledge?
5 Think carefully about how fire could have been created, then draw your own idea of what happened.

5 What's in a Name?

When babies are born, their parents give them names. It helps to avoid confusion. It means a person knows if you are talking to them. Most of our names mean something and for some people, the names they give their baby are very important. In fact, they are symbols.

The former heavyweight boxer, Cassius Clay, was named after a slave-owner. He changed his name to Muhammad Ali, a Muslim name. The name Muhammad means *praiseworthy*. The picture below shows what some other first names mean.

Fisher, Little and Hunter. Even surnames have meanings.

The Yoruba tribe of Nigeria takes great care with this. Their babies are studied carefully to see if one of their **ancestors** has been reborn in the child.

They may discover this from the baby's appearance or from its behaviour. So a boy may be called *Babatunde* which means 'Father has returned'; and a girl may be given the name *Yetunde* ('Mother has returned').

They have lots of other special names for all kinds of different births. Twins are called *Taiwo* and *Kehinde*. *Kehinde* means the twin who arrived afterwards. There is a special name for a child born face down and even one for a baby with six fingers!

| happy (Hindu) | manly (Christian) | trustworthy (Muslim) | fair (Christian) | a flower (Hindu) | lively (Jewish) |

Hindu parents seek advice before choosing a name for their child. When a Hindu baby is born, the parents will ask a priest or an **astrologer** to draw up a **horoscope** for it. It will be based on where the baby was born and on the exact moment it was born to make it as accurate as possible.

After he has studied the horoscope, the man will suggest some good names to the parents. Sometimes, the child will be given two names: one shows it has joined the living and the other shows it is now a member of a certain family.

For many people, the name they have is very important for religious reasons. So it is not surprising that the way people describe their god is also important. It shows how they think of him or her.

Perhaps this is most obvious in Hinduism. Hindus believe in many gods and some of these gods and goddesses can appear in more than one form. Below, you can see Parvati, the wife of the god Shiva. But she can also take the form of Uma, a beautiful young woman who sorts out disagreements between the gods.

Then, she is shown as Durga, the goddess of war. She rides on a lion's back and is armed for action! Finally, she is seen as Kali, the goddess of disease and fighting.

PARVATI   DURGA   KALI

1 Try to work out whether people's names affect you. Suppose you were told you had a new form tutor but you have not yet met the person. However, you have been told his or her name. How would you feel if it was (i) Mr Lazy; (ii) Mrs Windbag; or (iii) Miss Strict? Give reasons for your answers.

2 a) Look at the pictures of Kali and Durga. Describe what each one looks like.
b) Describe the feelings each of these pictures gives you.

3 Explain in your own words:
a) how Hindu parents choose a name for their child; and
b) why the child may have two names.

4 a) Describe the feelings each of these words gives you:
(i) Lord; (ii) Master; (iii) Father; (iv) King; and (v) Almighty.
b) How do *you* think of god?

5 a) In groups, discuss your names. Give each other any information you can. For instance, what does your name mean and why did your parents choose it?
b) If you have children when you are older, how will you choose names for them?
c) Would any of these names be symbols of anything? If so, explain what.

6 Remember, Remember …

This is the Cenotaph in London. It is a stone **monument** to remind us of the millions of people who died in the world wars. Every year, at 11 a.m. on the Sunday nearest 11 November, people lay wreaths beside it. They stand around it in silence for one minute and think of the dead.

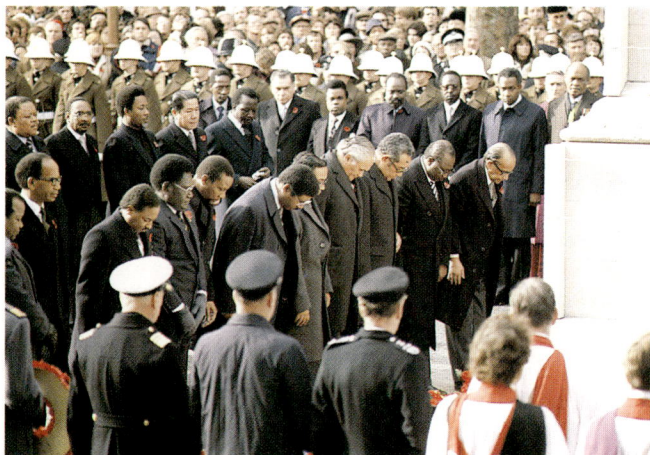

This monument is a symbol of people's suffering during those wars. The minute's silence is a symbol of people's respect for the dead. So are the wreaths. Even the time and date are symbolic. Eleven a.m. on 11 November was when the First World War ended.

People use different things to remind themselves of what they need to remember. Some people tie a knot in their handkerchief because they need to remember something. The knot does not tell them *what* to remember; it is only a symbol of *something* to remember.

Your homework, Jason?

Sorry, miss. I have to tie a knot in it or I'd forget it.

Followers of many religions use symbols in this way to remind them of their beliefs and to help them in their **devotion.** The most common symbol is the rosary which is a string of prayer beads. Strictly speaking, the rosary is the prayers which are counted on the beads. But people usually call the beads a rosary, too.

The old lady in the picture below is a Catholic. As she counts her rosary beads she **recites** the Lord's Prayer (once) the Hail Mary (ten times) and then finishes with a third prayer called the Gloria. These prayers will help to remind her of certain events in the life of Christ. Counting the beads will help her to concentrate.

Prayer beads similar to these are used in many religions. When Buddhists pray, they place the rosary round both their hands. It is a symbol that they are embracing the hand of Buddha.

There is no fixed number of beads for Buddhists, although some use a string of 108 beads. The beads themselves are symbols of the fifty-four stages which a Buddhist goes through in life before he or she reaches the state of Nirvana.

Muslims also use beads, but their beads symbolise something different. They stand for the 'ninety-nine names of God' which Muslims learn. So a full set of their beads contains ninety-nine.

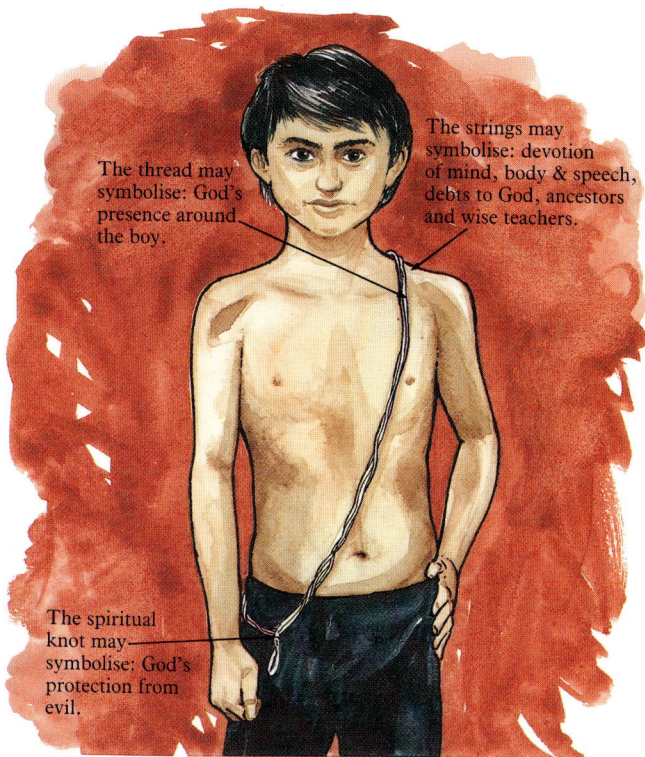

The thread may symbolise: God's presence around the boy.

The strings may symbolise: devotion of mind, body & speech, debts to God, ancestors and wise teachers.

The spiritual knot may symbolise: God's protection from evil.

A boy wearing the sacred thread. The captions show one way in which the strings act as symbols. Other Hindus say that the strings stand for the three main Hindu gods: Brahma, Vishnu and Shiva.

Prayer beads are things that a person can carry round with them to use at any time. However, some religions expect their followers to wear something which is a permanent symbol of their devotion to God.

Somewhere between the ages of eight and twelve, some Hindu boys go through a special ceremony, known as the Sacred Thread Ceremony. The number three is an important symbol in this. The thread has three strings, each containing three strands.

In a changing world, some Hindus today do not wear the sacred thread after the ceremony – or they wear it round their wrist instead. But the ceremony still occurs because it is a symbol in itself – a symbol that the child is committed to the Hindu faith and the Hindu way of life.

These words, spoken by the boy receiving the thread, show one way in which the thread is a symbol of three things:

▶ I submit to you to prepare me bodily.
Secondly, to give me the power to speak right thoughts; thirdly, to give me the power to think rightly for the sake of good.

This is part of a prayer said by the boy's father:

The natural source of the sacred thread is the Lord himself and it is bestowed again and again for **eternity**. It gives long life and favours thoughts of God. This thread I put round you. By the grace of God, may it give you power and brilliance.

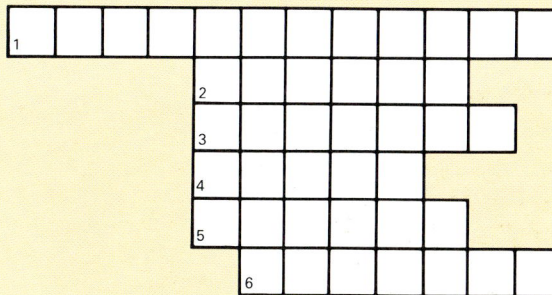

1 a) Copy out and complete this grid, using the clues below:
  (1) Tie a knot in it to help your memory!
  (2) Catholics say this prayer while counting their rosary.
  (3) These people have ninety-nine beads on their string.
  (4) Ninety-nine or 108 – they're all prayer _____ .
  (5) Hindus sometimes wear a sacred one.
  (6) What this book is all about.
  b) Now, find the word which reads downwards. Explain what it is and how it might be used.
2 a) Write down two things which people in Britain do to help remember people who have died.
  b) For each one, explain how it helps them to remember.
3 Write down something you have which reminds you of someone whom you rarely or never see any more. How does it remind you of them?
4 a) Draw someone wearing the sacred thread.
  b) Explain in full what the sacred thread can symbolise.

To Be a Pilgrim

The people below are Christian pilgrims. This means that they have set out on a journey to a holy place as a symbol of their devotion to God. They have reached their journey's end, at the little Norfolk town of Walsingham. Each Easter, its narrow streets are filled with people from all over the world.

Pilgrimages are less common in Britain now than they were many centuries ago. The speed of modern life leaves little time for such long journeys.

Elsewhere in the world, it is different. In Japan, Shinto followers still make their way up Mount Fuji. For them, the mountain is sacred and a **shrine** stands on its summit.

In India, many pilgrimage centres are linked to stories of the Hindu gods. Most sacred of all is Varanasi, a city built beside the River Ganges so that it faces the rising sun.

There are over 3000 temples in Varanasi and it is not just Hindus who travel there. Sikhs and Buddhists also visit it.

Muslims, too, have their own holiest city. It is Mecca, a city in Saudi Arabia. Muslims' holy book, the Qur'an, actually orders them to make a pilgrimage there at least once in their lives. However, sick or disabled people can ask someone to do it for them. Poor people can club together and send one person as a representative.

The journey itself is symbolic because Mecca was the birthplace of Muhammad, whom Muslims believe was God's greatest **prophet**. Many of the things which the Muslims do on their pilgrimage also involve symbols, as you can see opposite.

One visitor described the pilgrims at Varanasi:

▶ What unites the chanting crowds is the belief that, as they cup their hands and let the Ganga flow three times through their fingers, their sins are washed away.

Some pilgrims gain extra credit by filling bottles of the holy water to take home for those who cannot go. Afterwards, the pilgrims make their offerings to the river. Some will pour out milk or float dishes filled with yellow marigolds, or tiny oil lamps.

Pilgrims in the holy River Ganges at Varanasi, sometimes called Benares. The river is known by many names, including 'The Pure' and 'The cow which gives much milk'.

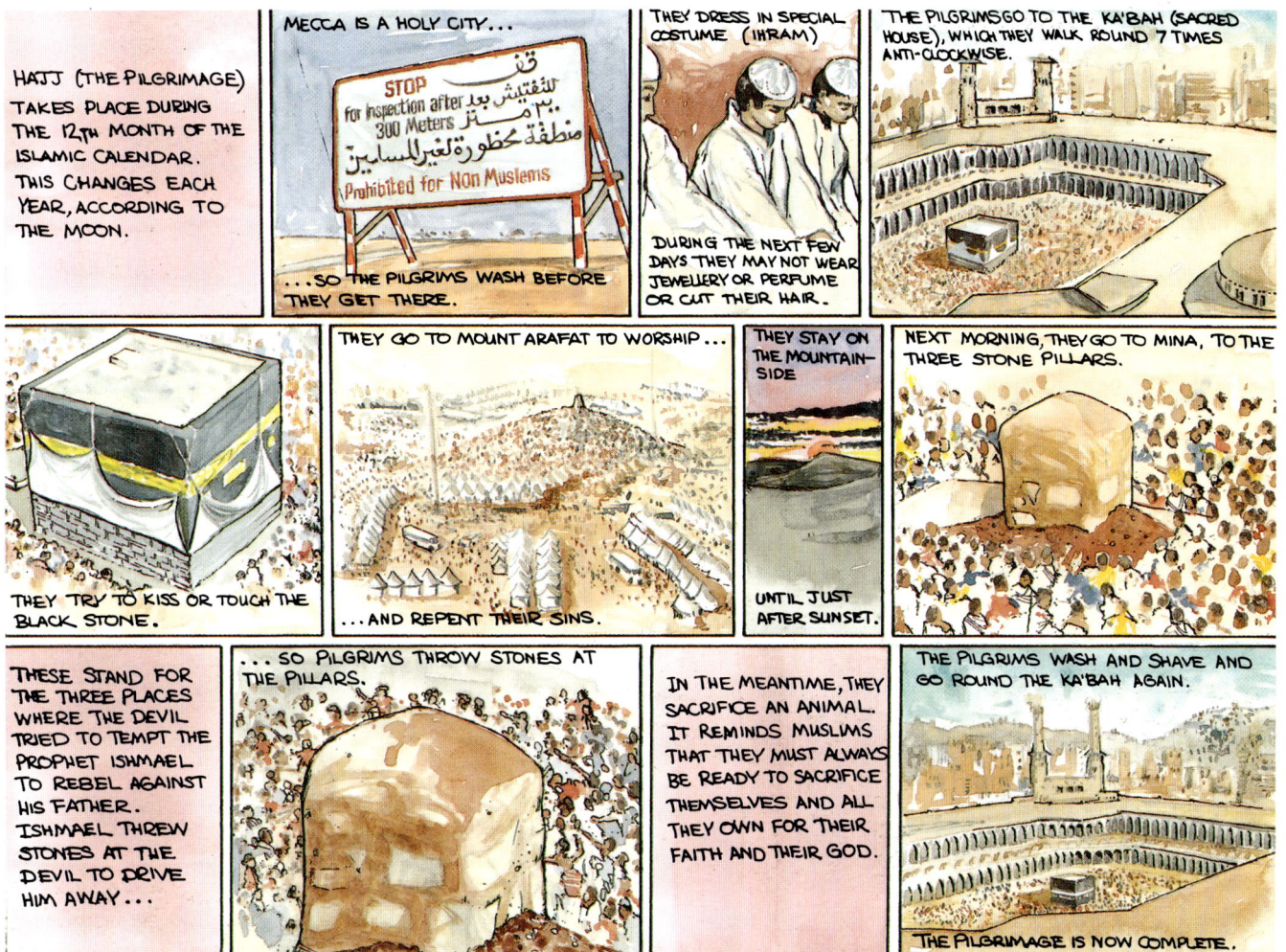

HAJJ (THE PILGRIMAGE) TAKES PLACE DURING THE 12TH MONTH OF THE ISLAMIC CALENDAR. THIS CHANGES EACH YEAR, ACCORDING TO THE MOON.

MECCA IS A HOLY CITY... STOP for inspection after 300 Meters Prohibited for Non Muslims ...SO THE PILGRIMS WASH BEFORE THEY GET THERE.

THEY DRESS IN SPECIAL COSTUME (IHRAM) DURING THE NEXT FEW DAYS THEY MAY NOT WEAR JEWELLERY OR PERFUME OR CUT THEIR HAIR.

THE PILGRIMS GO TO THE KA'BAH (SACRED HOUSE), WHICH THEY WALK ROUND 7 TIMES ANTI-CLOCKWISE.

THEY TRY TO KISS OR TOUCH THE BLACK STONE.

THEY GO TO MOUNT ARAFAT TO WORSHIP... ...AND REPENT THEIR SINS.

THEY STAY ON THE MOUNTAIN-SIDE UNTIL JUST AFTER SUNSET.

NEXT MORNING, THEY GO TO MINA, TO THE THREE STONE PILLARS.

THESE STAND FOR THE THREE PLACES WHERE THE DEVIL TRIED TO TEMPT THE PROPHET ISHMAEL TO REBEL AGAINST HIS FATHER. ISHMAEL THREW STONES AT THE DEVIL TO DRIVE HIM AWAY...

...SO PILGRIMS THROW STONES AT THE PILLARS.

IN THE MEANTIME, THEY SACRIFICE AN ANIMAL. IT REMINDS MUSLIMS THAT THEY MUST ALWAYS BE READY TO SACRIFICE THEMSELVES AND ALL THEY OWN FOR THEIR FAITH AND THEIR GOD.

THE PILGRIMS WASH AND SHAVE AND GO ROUND THE KA'BAH AGAIN. THE PILGRIMAGE IS NOW COMPLETE.

▶ And pilgrimage to the House is a duty people owe to God, for him who can afford the journey.
(Qur'an 3:97)

1 a) Explain the meanings of these words: pilgrimage; devotion; hajj; ihram; and repent.
b) Which religions use these places for pilgrimages: Mount Fuji; Varanasi; and Walsingham?
2 a) Why do Muslims believe they should go on a pilgrimage to Mecca?
b) Why do you think pilgrims to Varanasi sometimes take the river water home?
3 Look at the pictures above. The pilgrimage to Mecca involves many symbols.
a) Choose any three symbols and write down what the pilgrims do.
b) Explain what your three symbols stand for.
4 Which of the following words do you think might describe someone who had been on a pilgrimage to Mecca? (Give reasons for those you choose and add others, if you wish.)
happy; miserable; peaceful; clean; holy; contented; or fulfilled.
5 Christian pilgrims used to buy badges to show they had been on a pilgrimage. Draw a badge which would be suitable for any one of the pilgrimages mentioned on these two pages.

8 Houses of Prayer

Plan of a mosque.

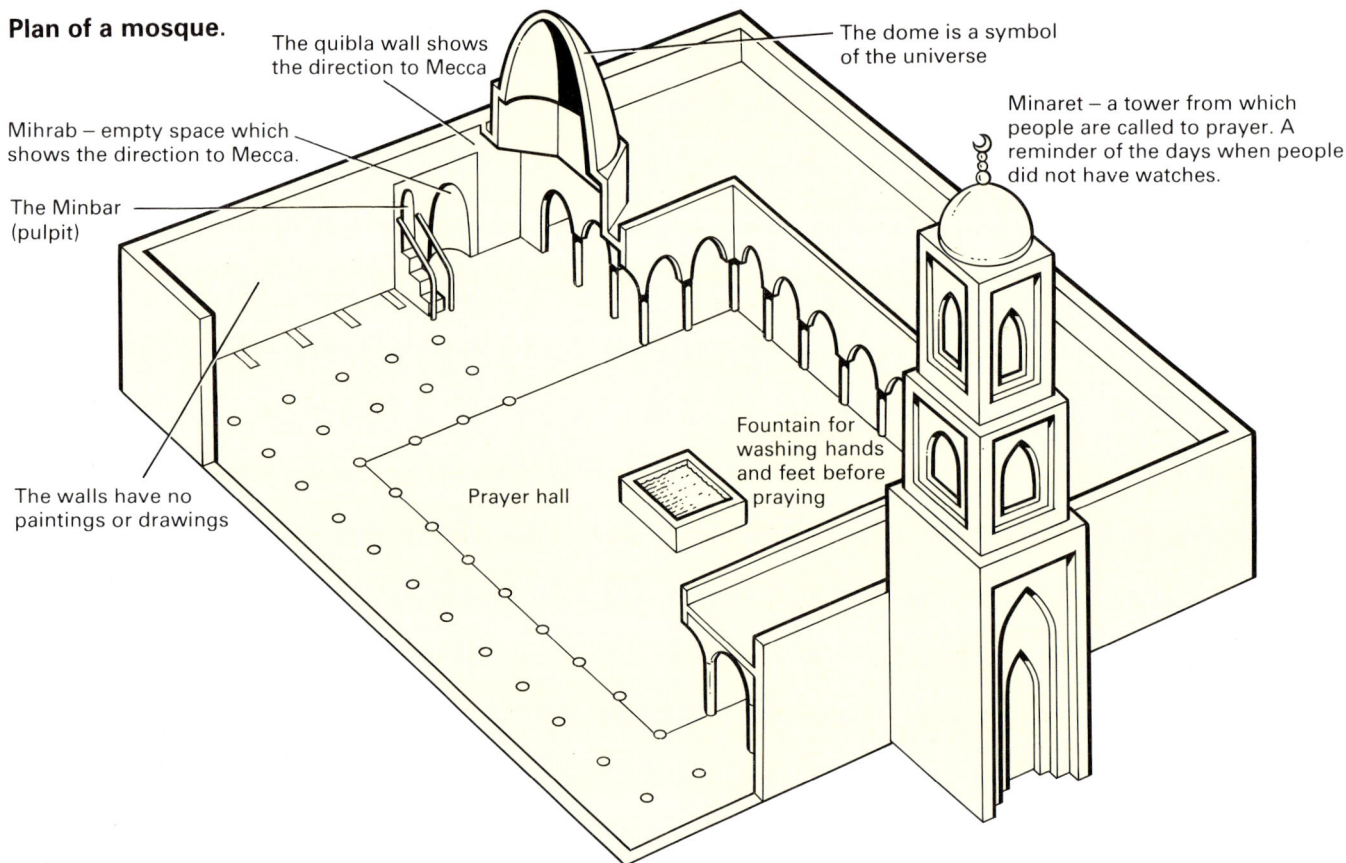

The quibla wall shows the direction to Mecca

The dome is a symbol of the universe

Mihrab – empty space which shows the direction to Mecca.

Minaret – a tower from which people are called to prayer. A reminder of the days when people did not have watches.

The Minbar (pulpit)

The walls have no paintings or drawings

Prayer hall

Fountain for washing hands and feet before praying

Muslims worship in a building called a mosque. It means 'a place of **prostration**'; in other words, somewhere where Muslims bow down low before God and pray to Him. It is a symbol of their **submission** to God. In fact, 'Muslim' means 'a person who submits to God'.

Even the way the building is built is symbolic. When Muslims pray, they face in the direction of Mecca. So each mosque is built with a hollow space in one wall to show people the exact direction of the holy city.

Inside, mosques are very bare. This, too, is symbolic. There are no pictures of God because Muslims believe it is wrong to try to paint or draw Him. There are no pictures of animals or plants, either.

Muslims believe that it is God's work to create; it is not a job for human beings. Instead, the mosque contains patterns of beautiful lettering on the ceiling and pillars. This comes from the Qur'an.

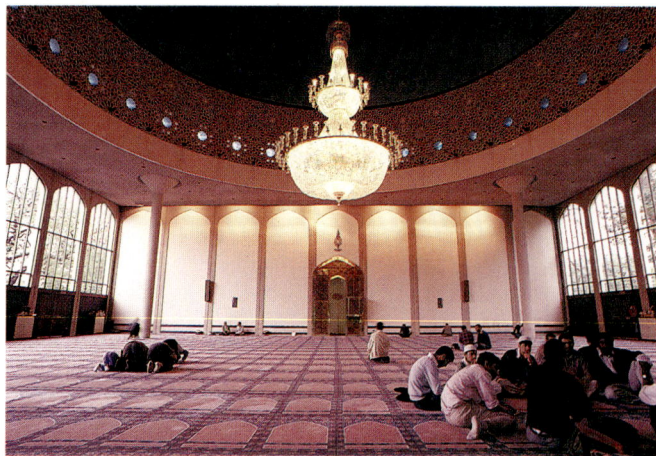

Regents Park mosque in London. It cost nearly six million pounds to build. A plan of a more typical mosque is shown at the top of the page.

The Greek Cathedral St Sophia in London. The huge hanging cross has ruby lamps which are lit on special occasions. The holy table is a symbol of God's presence. The iconostasis (icon-screen) is a symbol of the division between heaven and earth.

cross, with a dome high above it. In the dome is a picture of Christ, surrounded by angels or the **Apostles**.

Each Greek Orthodox church has two large paintings of Jesus, as well as twelve smaller ones, showing scenes from his life. These are called icons. When someone goes into the church, they will kiss the icon in the entrance and bow before it. They usually also buy a candle and place it before the icon.

Just behind the icon-screen are the royal doors. The centre door is opened during services as a symbol that man can enter into God's presence.

Light is a very important symbol in Orthodox churches. Two large candle-holders stand in front of the icon-screen. The candles are lit as a symbol of devotion to God and of respect for the Saints.

High above, chandeliers represent the stars in the sky; they also remind Christians of God whom they call the 'Father of Light'. The caption explains some of the church's other symbols.

There are Christians living in all parts of the world today. They all believe in the same God but they do not all worship in the same way. And their churches come in all shapes and sizes.

The picture above shows a Greek Orthodox Christian church in London. These churches are common in Greece itself but there are only about twenty of them in Britain.

The shape is symbolic. It is based on a Greek

1 Match up the words on the left with the correct description from the right.

minbar	Muslim holy book
mosque	Muslim holy city
Qur'an	Muslim place of worship
Mecca	one who submits to God's will
Muslim	pulpit in a mosque

2 Explain what each of the following symbolises to a Muslim: (i) the bare walls of a mosque; (ii) bowing down low to God; (iii) facing in the direction of Mecca to pray.

3 a) List the differences between a mosque and a Greek Orthodox church.
   b) Why do you think the Greek church has so many pictures in it?

4 Visit the religious building which is nearest to your school. Try to talk to someone who works there and ask them about the building's symbols. Then, draw a plan of the building and mark any symbols on it.

9 *Food for Thought*

The picture above does not need a caption. You just know that it shows a little girl blowing out the candles on her birthday cake. How do you know? Probably the candles are the best clue. Each one is a symbol of a year in the girl's life.

Most food which British people eat is not symbolic. But, for some religious groups, it is different. Look at the Jewish family below. What day do you think it is? And what time of day is it?

Most Jewish people would know at once by looking at the shape of the bread. The family is beginning the Sabbath, their day of rest, which begins on Friday evening.

Part of this meal is the two loaves of bread, called hallot. They have a special shape and are only eaten on the Sabbath. It is a reminder of an event in the past and the caption explains its symbols.

A Jewish family begin their Friday evening meal at the start of Sabbath. At the meal there are *two loaves*, a symbol of the double helping of Manna which God gave the Jews in the Wilderness, ready for the Sabbath. The *loaves are plaited*, a symbol of a bride's wreath and a reminder that the Sabbath is seen as a 'bride'. The *coverlet* is a symbol of the dew on the manna.

Hot cross buns Christians used them as symbols of the new life of Jesus. In the middle ages, Christians were not allowed to eat them during Lent, so they were a special Easter treat.

Christians believed that you went without fine food and drink during Lent, which meant using up all the butter and eggs on the day before – and you make this food with those ingredients.

Leeks

Easter eggs

In ancient times, people ate small wheat-cakes at their spring festivals. Their shape was a symbol of the full moon and its four quarters. Christians ate the cakes on Good Friday, as a symbol of the death of Jesus on the cross.

Various foods which are symbolic. The captions explain the symbols. See question 5 below.

Pancakes These are the symbol of the Welsh people. Legend has it that they were eaten by St David and his monks.

In many countries, sharing bread is a symbol of friendship, rather like sharing out your birthday cake. But it can also mean much more than this. Christians have a special service, called Holy Communion or Mass. Part of this involves people in the **congregation** being given a small piece of bread and a sip of wine. (In Catholic churches, only the priest has the wine.)

Eating the bread and drinking the wine are important acts, but not because the people are hungry – or because the food is specially good. It is what the bread and wine stand for that is important.

It reminds Christians of the last meal which Jesus ate with his **disciples**. They call it the Last Supper. There was bread and wine at this meal. The Bible describes what happened:

▶ The Lord Jesus … took a piece of bread, gave thanks to God, broke it, and said, 'This is my body, which is for you. Do this in memory of me.' In the same way, after the supper he took the cup and said, 'This cup is God's new **covenant,** sealed with my blood. Whenever you drink it, do so in memory of me.' (1 Corinthians 11: 23–25)

So when Christians take bread and wine at Communion, it is a symbol of the Last Supper. But it is more than that. The wine itself is a symbol of the blood of Jesus, and the bread is a symbol of his body. And both are a symbol of his suffering when he died on the cross.

1 Copy out and complete this paragraph:
   Jewish people begin their _____ on Friday and it ends on _____ . On Friday evening, they have a meal which includes two loaves of bread, called _____ . These have a special shape.
2 Look at the photograph of the Jewish family. Write down the three symbols you can see in the picture and explain what each one stands for.
3 a) Write down any two foods which remind you of special events and explain what they remind you of. (Please don't choose birthday cake!)

   b) At the end of the lesson, you could each read out your answers. See if other people can guess what they remind you of.
4 a) Why do you think *bread* is a good symbol of sharing?
   b) Why don't people use food like baked beans instead? (Think hard!)
5 Look at the drawings above of different symbolic foods and read the captions. Write down the name of each food. Then, write down the caption which you think fits that food.
6 Design your own symbol to show the idea of (i) sharing or (ii) Holy Communion.

10 All Dressed Up

Many people wear special clothes for the job they do. Sometimes, it is something like a pair of overalls just to keep them clean. But others wear a uniform so that people will know who they are. You can usually recognise a bus driver or a policeman because of their uniform, and that's why they wear it.

The same is true in many religions. However, it is not always easy to tell which clothes are worn for symbolic reasons and which ones are worn for some other reason, such as fashion.

Think of weddings. Many Christian women today like to get married in a white dress, which is a symbol of **purity**. But the custom of white weddings only goes back to the nineteenth century. In Roman times, for instance, yellow was the popular colour.

Hindu brides usually get married in a red **sari**. The marriage is an important ceremony because Hindus believe it is a duty to carry on your family. The bride spends days getting ready for

Although this is a modern Japanese wedding the bride still wears a **Kimono**. Her head covering is a symbol of hiding her jealousy.

the big day. When it is over, she will probably wear a wedding ring to show that she is married; some Hindu women also wear special toe rings.

While Hindu women wear special make-up to show that they are married, Muslim women do not wear make-up in public at all. The Qur'an says that women should not wear any 'ornaments' in public. So they do not wear jewellery, except at home. There, a Muslim woman can wear what she likes, including jewellery and make-up.

The Qur'an also asks them not to display their bodies in a way which will attract men. So, many Muslim women wear a costume which covers their whole body, except for their hands and face. The clothes must be loose-fitting, too, so that men are not attracted by the shape of their body.

Like Hindu women, many Chinese women used to get married in red clothes because the Chinese thought it was a lucky and joyful colour. However, earlier this century, a Japanese bride often wore a white dress when saying good-bye

The two faces of Muslim women. Some Muslim women now wear western-style clothes but others still keep their bodies covered. Some women cover their faces, too. Experts still argue about whether this is necessary or not. The woman in the long robe may still be wearing western clothes underneath.

> ▶ O Prophet, tell your wives and daughters and the women of the believers to draw upon them their over-garments. That is more appropriate so that they may be recognised and not **molested.** (Qur'an 33:59)

to her parents because it was a sign of mourning.

Perhaps that seems odd on her wedding day! But the idea was that she was 'dying' to her own parents – and also that she would never leave her husband's house until she, too, died. The last thing she would dream of wearing was purple because it fades so easily. That might be a sign that the marriage would not last!

A Hindu woman gets ready for her marriage. The tilaka (red spot) shows that she is blessed. She will wear make-up on her hands and feet which leaves the skin dyed red for weeks. She will also wear the best gold jewellery she can afford. A married Hindu woman nearby wears a tali – a jewel set in gold, knotted by a short string. The knot is a symbol of possession. Heavy eye make-up, made of **ghee** and lampblack, was originally worn to keep flies away.

Divine Images

We asked a group of primary school children to draw us a picture of God. The pictures above show what they came up with. They are all different but they have one key feature in common. Each picture looks like a human being.

Many people think the same way. They believe that gods look rather like themselves.

Two pictures of Jesus, one from Italy and one from the Arctic. The picture on the left shows a **nativity** scene, with Mary holding the baby Jesus and Joseph in the background. The picture above is of Jesus as the good shepherd.

Often, when they make statues of their gods, they look after them, just as if they were looking after a human being.

Hindus dress statues of their gods in beautiful clothes and cool them with water when it is hot. They even give them gifts of food. Of course, these statues are not real portraits of the gods because no one can know what a god looks like.

So they are symbols. The clothes they wear and even the way they look is a kind of message, reminding people of how their God or gods can act. However, among African tribes, images of a **supreme** God are rare, although there are lots of images of less important ones. Many Africans just do not think you can make a picture of God.

Some other religions teach that it is wrong even to try. If we had asked Jewish or Muslim children to paint God, they would have been shocked. Jewish children learn the Ten **Commandments**. This is the second of them:

> ▶ Do not make for yourselves images of anything in heaven or on earth or in the water under the earth.

Muslims are not allowed to make images of people or creatures, which is why they decorate their mosques with patterns and writing. However, in the past, Persian Muslims did not follow the rule as strictly as Muslims elsewhere.

There is no Christian ban on pictures of Jesus.

Indeed, most churches contain paintings and statues and even pictures in stained glass windows. But the artists still tend to make pictures which look like themselves.

Chinese Christians have paintings of a Chinese-looking Christ. Even the angels look Chinese. But in Africa, the Virgin Mary is shown with an African hair-style and the wise men wear flowing African robes.

Even the symbols are different. The same person may be shown in different situations or doing different things. The photographs on page 24 are an example of this.

Statues of Buddha, the founder of Buddhism, are full of symbols. They are usually huge to show that, although he was an ordinary person, he was spiritually higher than other people. The dot between the eyebrows is a symbol of an inward eye; the long ear lobes are symbolic of spiritual wisdom. Even the positions of his hands and body are symbolic.

1 Read the four statements below and decide which might have been made by (i) a Christian; (ii) a Jew; (iii) a Buddhist and (iv) a Muslim. For each one, explain how you decided.

(a) We believe that only God can create so it would be wrong for us to make pictures of animals.
(b) As he is spiritually higher, he is often shown larger than life-size.
(c) The second commandment says it is wrong to draw or paint people.
(d) I see Him as the good shepherd, looking after people, who are his flock.

2 a) All the children drew God as a man. Why do you think they did that?
b) If your religion allows it, draw your own idea of God.

3 a) Look at the two photos on page 24 and read the caption. Which picture is Italian and which picture is the Eskimo one? Give reasons for your answers.
b) Why do you think one artist drew sheep?
c) What is Joseph doing in the picture on the left?

4 Think of how an African might draw the birth of Jesus. Then, design a Christmas card which includes such a picture.

12 *Symbols in Dance and Drama*

▶ This is what happens during a dervish dance: each dervish starts spinning on the spot. Gradually, he opens up, by raising one hand to heaven to receive divine grace while, with the other hand lowered, he passes this grace on to the earth. Little by little, he spins faster as if, by his turning, he links heaven and earth.

The dervish is supposed to make this contact by bringing the spirit down through his own body to the ground, while his own heart is unmoving, and his mind soars to its divine source.

Each dancer whirls around on the spot, like a planet. At the same time, he turns in the group around a radiant sun, represented by the Sheik. As they progress, their spirits spiral up, finally making a union with the divine.

It comes to an end as abruptly as a dream. It lasted several hours but the ecstasy was fleeting. For the last time, the music of the flute sings out the suffering of man, cut off from God. Slowly, the dervish regains awareness of his condition.

The men above are doing more than just dancing. They are remembering God and their dance helps them to do so. These dancers are Muslims, living in Turkey, and called the Mevlevi. However, Europeans know them better as whirling dervishes. It is a Turkish word which means 'poor people'.

As they dance, they repeat words which remind them of God, just as other Muslims might count their prayer beads. They believe it brings them into more direct contact with God; in fact, they claim that their dancing is the work of God.

The Hindu god Shiva is shown in various ways. In the picture above, he is shown as the Lord of the Dance. The dancing is a symbol of energy in the world and the god's arms are an extension of his own energy. The drum in one of his right hands is a symbol of creation while his other right hand symbolises peace. The creature under his feet is a symbol of ignorance; the fact that he is dancing on top of it is also a symbol.

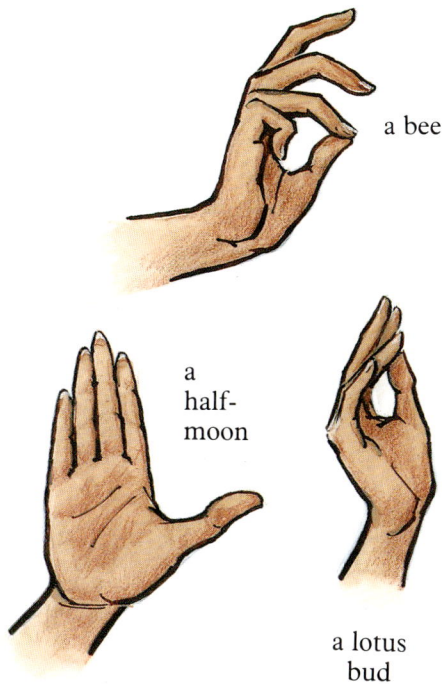

a bee

a half-moon

a lotus bud

Hand symbols used in Indian dancing.

The dervishes are a special religious group, but dancing is a normal part of many religions. People can dance to praise God or to ask him for a gift; they can dance for joy or to show their sadness; or they can dance to act out stories of their gods. The dancing helps people to understand their religion better and feel closer to their gods.

Most Africans could not imagine their religion without dancing. Every year, the Ife tribe in Nigeria hold a festival for their God Obatala. On most days during the festival, people dance through the streets in procession.

On the third day, as a **sacrifice** ends, the tribal drums start beating and everyone starts dancing. As they dance, the priests sing, 'God sees this gathering'. Then, the chiefs dance seven times around the **compound**. Each time, there is a different dance and a different song. The festival would not be complete without it.

According to one Hindu version of the

creation, it was only when the gods danced that life really began on earth. So it is not surprising that many of their gods are sometimes pictured dancing. Even the god of war has his own victory dance.

But the best-known of the dancing gods is Shiva, the Lord of the Dance. He is also one of the most popular of the Hindu gods. The statue on page 26 shows him dancing. It is also a mass of symbols. In fact, even the dance itself is a symbol.

His followers believe that dance is a symbol of energy. This energy creates everything in the world – plants, animals and people, but it also destroys things. Plants grow, have flowers and then die. But the seeds create new plants which will also eventually wither and die.

The process never ends. As long as there is life, things will be born and will die. So the statue shows that, too. The flames around the outside stand for these deaths. The circle stands for time. It has no beginning and it has no end.

1 a) Look at the picture of Shiva and read what is written about him on this page. Write down at least three things you can see in the picture.
   b) Write down what each of these things symbolises. (Some answers are on this page; try to work out what any of the others mean.)
2 Look at the picture of the dervishes and read the description of a dervish dance. Write down at least three ways in which the writing adds to your understanding of their dances.
3 Draw a mask which would be suitable for one of these gods: a god of war; a god of music; a sun god; a kitchen god. Write a few sentences to explain why you drew it as you did.
4 Look at the hand symbols above. As a group, think of good ways of using your hands to show (i) the sun rising; (ii) happiness; (iii) you are thanking someone; (iv) you are praising God.
5 People in Britain do not usually dance in churches. Why do you think that is?

13 New Beginnings

It is late January in Manchester. There is red paper decorating the houses and soon, red fireworks will be exploding. Everyone, especially the children, is getting excited. The New Year is about to begin.

New Year? Don't people usually think of the New Year as starting at midnight on 31 December? There is a simple answer. For most people in Britain, New Year *does* begin on 1 January – but not for the Chinese.

In fact, the Chinese New Year does not even start on the same day each year. It may be in January or February; it all depends on the movements of the moon.

However, the preparations begin long before. Sacrifices are offered to the kitchen god and his portrait is put on the kitchen wall. The family offers him malt sugar, hoping that he will say good things about them when he reports back to heaven. Meanwhile, the hearth is made shining clean, ready for his return.

It is decorated with red paper, too. For the Chinese, red is a symbol of good luck. It keeps the gods happy. Even the red fireworks are symbols. They show people's respect for the gods – and scare away the **demons!**

Late at night, when the fireworks begin, the air is filled with a sweet smell. People have started lighting **joss-sticks** to welcome the spirits of their ancestors coming to earth.

And that's just the start! Two weeks of celebrations are about to begin, with something different going on most nights. It will all end on the night of a full moon.

Then, everyone goes into the street to watch or join in the great parade. There is music, singing and dancing – and a long dragon, carried on men's shoulders. People offer him money, wrapped in red paper.

In front of the dragon, men roll a huge ball, made of yellow silk. It is a symbol of the sun. If the dragon catches the sun, he will put it out. But he doesn't. Instead, the crowd catches him and burns him on a bonfire. Another year has begun; people have made yet another new beginning.

Most people make a new start at some stage of their life, even if it only means a new year's **resolution**. On the island of Bali, people make one of the most spectacular new beginnings of all – and it only happens once in a hundred years.

The last time was in 1979. The Balinese

people spent two months getting ready for Eka Dasa Rudra. The reason for the event is to get rid of all the wrongs which have built up over the last 100 years.

This altar is built by the sea as part of the festival.

A large part of this ceremony involves sacrifices, including sacrifices to the spirit of Mount Agung, the great volcano which rises in the heart of the island. One evening, at dusk, a buffalo is thrown into the crater as an offering to the Earth God; another buffalo is sacrificed to the God of the Sea.

But one of the biggest events is arranged to allow the spirits of Bali's animals to join the gods. A great number of creatures are sacrificed at the sacred temple, at the base of the volcano – a buffalo, pig, cat, dog, eagle, pigeon, spider, and even a flea.

One of each kind of creature on the island has to die. Each sacrifice makes sure that the rest of their kind will survive on the island, at least for the next 100 years. Afterwards, there is much dancing and singing as the people of Bali celebrate their very special new beginning.

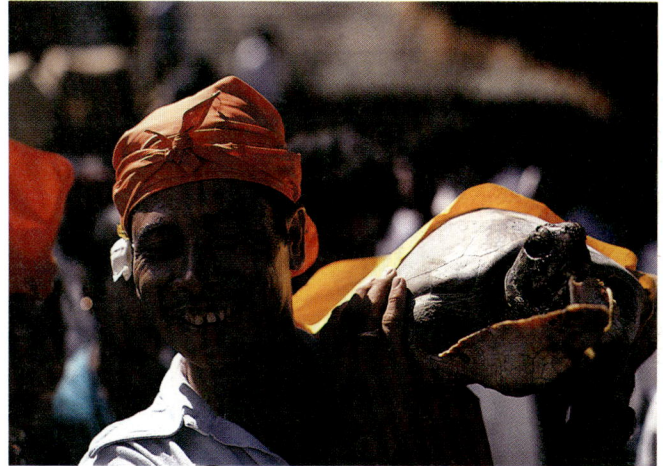
This turtle is just one of the creatures being taken to die.

For this book, though, we have nearly reached the end – but even that may prove to be just a beginning! The understanding you have gained should be with you for the rest of your lifetime. And *that* will involve a whole lot of new beginnings!

1 Explain the meanings of each of these words:
  demon; sacrifice; celebration; joss-stick.
2 Write down the symbols involved in the Chinese New Year events and explain what each one stands for. You should be able to find at least five.
3 a) Describe what your family does on New Year's Day. Do you do anything symbolic?
  b) Write down any New Year's resolutions your family has made. Have they managed to keep them?
4 a) How do the people of Bali mark the beginning of a new century?
  b) Explain why sacrifices are so important to them at this time.
5 If you had to imagine a god of the New Year, what would he or she look like? Draw a suitable picture of this god and explain why you drew him or her like that.
6 The Romans had a god called Janus who gave his name to January. Look up a picture of him in the library. Do you think he looks better than your New Year god or not? Give reasons for your answer.

Connections

8 AS A BOY, I WENT THROUGH THE SACRED THREAD CEREMONY
2 IN THE DOME OF OUR CHURCH IS A PAINTING OF CHRIST
9 HOLY COMMUNION REMINDS ME OF THE LAST SUPPER
6 WE SACRIFICE ANIMALS TO OUR SACRED MOUNTAIN
10 WE HAVE GODS OF THE SUN, MOON AND STARS
4 OUR SYMBOL INCLUDES A TWO-EDGED SWORD
7 OUR SABBATH BEGINS ON FRIDAY EVENING
5 OUR SYMBOL IS THE WHEEL OF THE LAW
3 WHEN I PRAY, I TURN TOWARDS MECCA
1 THE HORSE IS A HOLY ANIMAL FOR US

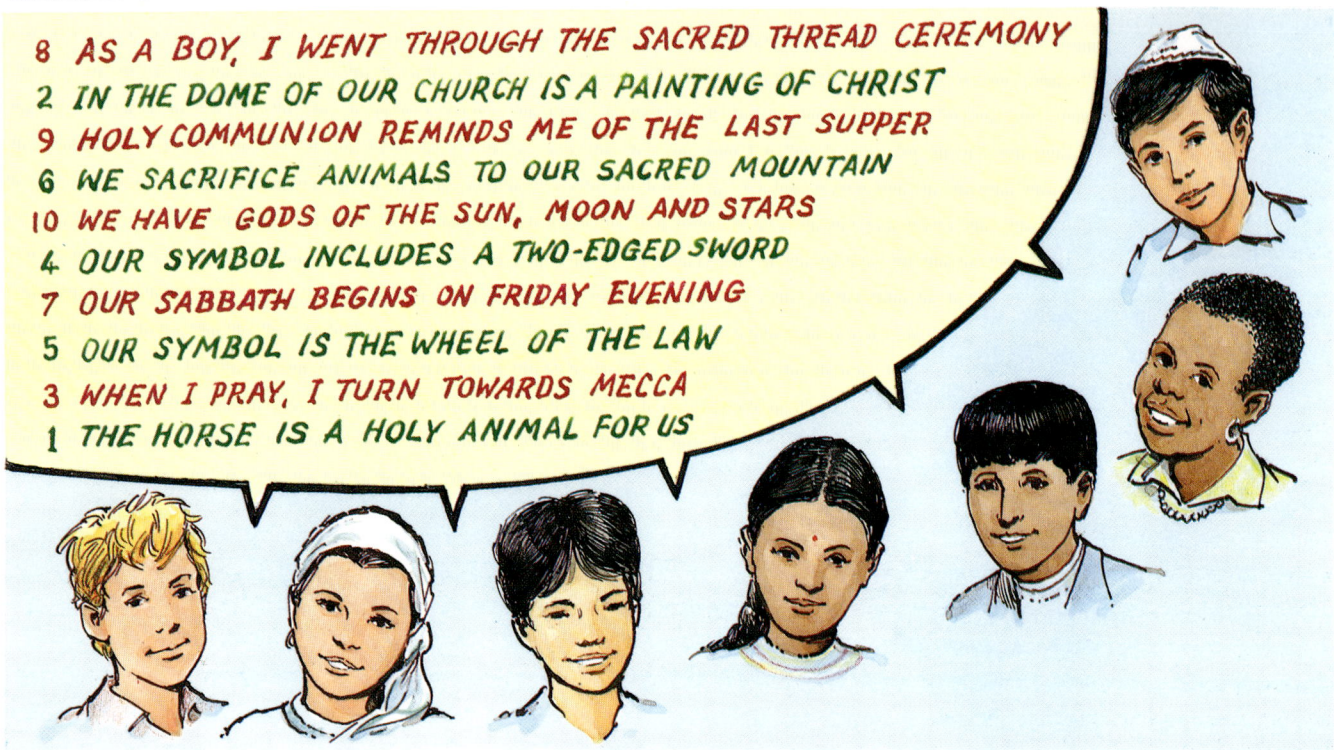

1 Who said what?
Draw the grid below in your exercise book, using a pencil and ruler. Next, look at what the people above are saying. Your job is to work out who said what. For example, if you think a Muslim would have said, 'Our symbol is the Wheel of the Law', put a tick beside the Muslim in column 1. But be careful! Three of the ten people speaking are not on the list!

	1	2	3	4	5	6	7	8	9	10
Muslim										
Buddhist										
Christian										
Jew										
Sikh										
Hindu										
Greek Orthodox Christian										

2 The crossword with no clues.
Copy out the grid below. Then, complete each word by using two letters from anywhere in the box on the right. All the words have been used in this book.

S	Y			O	L	█
I	S			M	█	█
	D		M	█	█	█
K	H	A		D	█	█
P	A		V	A	T	
R		S	A	R	█	█
N		R	V	A	N	
P	I	L			I	M

A	G
R	A
R	O
A	A
N	B
A	M
I	I
L	Y

3 You have reached the end of our book on symbols and the obvious way to end it is by drawing a symbol to show that it is all over! Design your own symbol for the end of this book. You could even hold a competition to decide which of all your symbols your group thinks is best.

Glossary

ancestor – person from whom one is descended, such as one's father or grandfather

Apostles – the twelve men chosen by Christ to spread his teaching to the world

astrologer – person who claims to know how the stars can influence people, especially in the future

Commandment – one of the ten laws of Moses in the Old Testament

compound – enclosure for a group of people

congregation – people who have come together to worship

covenant – agreement

coverlet – small covering

creation – the act of making the world

demon – devil or evil spirit

devotion – giving oneself up to the service of God

disciple – one of the followers of Jesus

eternity – for ever without end

ghee – pure butter

horoscope – diagram of the heavens used in telling fortunes

joss-stick – stick of gum burned for the gods, with a sweet smell of incense

kimono – loose garment worn by Japanese

Lent – the forty week-days before Easter

luminous – shining by its own light

manna – food

Mihrab – recess in wall in mosque facing Mecca

molested – interfered with and disturbed

monument – building which reminds people of a person or event

myth – made-up story with a meaning

nativity – birth

nirvana – the end of individual existence (a state which Buddhists try to achieve)

nuclear disarmament – getting rid of nuclear weapons, such as the atom bomb

ornament – anything pretty which adds beauty

patron saint – saint who guards and looks after a country or certain people

pollution – dirt

prophet – person who preaches what has been revealed to him (usually by God)

prostration – bowing down low or lying face down

purity – innocence

Ramadan – month during which Muslims fast in the daytime

recite – say aloud from memory

repent – ask for forgiveness for sin

resolution – something you have firmly decided

sacrifice – offering to a god

sari – a long cloth worn by a Hindu woman; it is wrapped round the waist and passed over the shoulder

sash – long strip of cloth or ribbon

shrine – sacred place

submission – obedience to power

supreme – greatest or most important

Index